911...

WHAT'S YOUR EMERGENCY?

DO NOT CROSS CRIME SCENE DO NOT CROSS CRIME SCENE DO NOT CROSS CRIM

MARK AGAN

911...What's Your Emergency?

Find more books by Mark Agan at: www.MarkAgan.com

ISBN-13: 978-1479234523
Printed in the United States of America

CONTENTS

INTRODUCTION

"9-1-1...What's your emergency?"

I hope I *never* have to hear those words in real life. Why? Because it would mean something bad had happened. Let's face it. When a person calls 9-1-1 they are not calling to share good news.

When the 9-1-1 operator answers the telephone it is usually a matter of life and death. Well, what you are about to read could be a matter of life or death, *spiritually.*

"Come on, now. Is it really THAT serious?" Evidently Jesus thought so because He said, *"And fear not them which kill the body, but are not able to kill the soul: but rather fear him which is able to destroy both soul and body in hell."* (Matt. 10:28)

Jesus was saying that between the two, you should be more concerned with your **soul** which is *eternal* than with your **body** which is only *temporal*.

So let's see what the emergency is all about.

CHAPTER 1

Is It A Self-Inflicted Wound?

"I don't think she's going to make it!" they yelled as they transported her to the hospital.

This was no ordinary injury. In fact, it was probably one of the most *unusual* injuries the emergency medical team had ever seen. How could this have happened to a young lady with such a promising career?

OK. Maybe I need to start from the beginning.

That day began like any other day. It was almost Christmas time which was evident by the brightly colored lights everywhere.

She was a beautiful young model named Lauren Scruggs. She and some friends decided to go flying in an airplane that night to see the Christmas lights. After the flight, they landed and as they were leaving the plane Lauren turned the wrong way and walked right into the plane's propeller!

As you can imagine, she suffered multiple injuries including losing her left eye and severing her left hand. In only a matter of seconds, what began as a fun-filled adventure quickly turned into a life-threatening scene.

Accidents like this are always tragic but what makes them even *more* tragic is when they are self-inflicted injuries. It would be a horrible thing to endure the pain and trauma of such an injury, but worse still would be to know that you did it to yourself!

While it is sad to say, the misery that many are experiencing in their lives is misery they have brought upon themselves. It is SELF-INFLICTED! We make bad choices and then must suffer the painful consequences.

The self-inflicted wound is the most difficult kind of wound for us to understand. The reason that it is difficult to understand is because we know that life itself is going to inflict a certain amount of sorrow and suffering on us already.

Man that is born of a woman is of few days, and full of trouble. (Job 14:1)

Suffering is not something we need to go looking for, it will find us! If you live very long at all in this world, you will encounter suffering. But while most of us do everything we can to keep it from finding us, there are some who seek it. They actually seek to hurt themselves. There are several ways people hurt themselves.

People Hurt Themselves PHYSICALLY

Those who practice "self-injury" are often people who feel they deserve such treatment.

For example, there are many women who are abused and beaten by their husbands but they do not flee from this abusive marriage because they somehow feel they are getting what they deserve. You can ask them, and they will tell you, "It really isn't his fault, I provoked the conflict."

3

I have been in psychiatric wards to visit people who have tried to harm themselves because they felt they deserved it.

People Hurt Themselves EMOTIONALLY

Some believe that their worth is wrapped up in what *others* think of them while others believe that their worth is wrapped up in what they *think of themselves.*

Our worth is not found in either one of these. If we have trusted in Jesus Christ as our Savior, our worth is wrapped up in who we are in Christ. When we realize we have been: regenerated by the Spirit of God, placed into the family of God, forgiven of all sin, and have eternal life and a home in heaven...THAT IS ENOUGH IDENTITY FOR ANYONE!!!

What has happened is they have bought into the world's philosophy that before you can truly love someone else you must first love yourself. The problem with this philosophy it that it is not scriptural!

Christ said in Matthew 22:37 that the whole law could be summed up in two commandments:

love God with all your heart and love your neighbor as yourself. Yet some Christians are not satisfied with that. They feel they need to add a third commandment to the Word of God: **thou shalt love thyself!**

So why doesn't the Bible tell us to first love ourselves? This is why: the Bible presupposes that men already love themselves far too much! You do not have to teach a person to love themselves. A child does not have to be taught to be selfish. If anything, a child must be taught NOT to be selfish.

We hold grudges toward others, but never toward ourselves. In fact, we give ourselves the benefit of the doubt, when we do not do so to others. We find this same teaching in Ephesians 5 where Paul urges men to love their wives as they love their own bodies.

So ought men to love their wives as their own bodies. He that loveth his wife loveth himself. (Eph. 5:28)

Paul did not say men must first love their own bodies before they can love their wives. He assumes that men already love themselves.

For no man ever yet hated his own flesh; but nourisheth and cherisheth it, even as the Lord the church: (Eph. 5:29)

So the scriptural view is, "love others and **then** you will love yourself." Because of this misunderstood principle, there are many folks out there hurting and the sad thing about it is they are doing it to themselves. What Jesus was saying is that we must learn to have the same intense love for others that we have developed for ourselves.

D.L. Moody said, "I picture the world as a wrecked vessel, drawing nearer and nearer to destruction. God gave me a lifeboat and said, 'Here, Moody, save all you can.'"

People Hurt Themselves SPIRITUALLY

What many people do not realize is that much of the conflict that is in the home they bring on themselves. The Bible says in Psalm 7:16, *"His mischief shall return upon his own head..."* Over and over again the Bible clearly teaches that we will reap what we sow.

Be not deceived; God is not mocked: for whatsoever a man soweth, that shall he also reap. (Gal. 6:7)

6

Someone said it this way, "You can't give birth to sin without having to live with the baby!" In other words, you can't have your sin without the consequences of that sin. Yes, God in His GRACE forgives but God in His GOVERNMENT says you must reap what you sow.

So a husband hurts himself spiritually when he does not love and honor his wife. A wife hurts herself AND the children spiritually by not following the leadership of her husband. Children are hurting themselves spiritually by not obeying their parents and those in authority.

God gave us the Bible, His instruction manual for the way we are to live our lives. He also gave us the church, a place where we can come and hear the Bible preached and taught and learn what God says about how to live.

Ironically, the very place God gave to help us live happy, blessed lives is the first place many people avoid when things begin falling apart.

To avoid God, the Bible, and church when things are going wrong makes about as much sense as avoiding the hospital when it is a matter of life and death!

Jesus came to help us

Some people try to avoid Jesus as if He is going to *hurt* them when the truth is, He came to *help* them! The Bible tells us that when Jesus was on earth He went about doing good.

> *How God anointed Jesus of Nazareth with the Holy Ghost and with power: who went about **doing good**, and healing all that were oppressed of the devil; for God was with him. (Acts 10:38)*

In fact, Jesus did so many good things and miracles that John said, *"And there are also many other things which Jesus did, the which, if they should be written every one, I suppose that even the world itself could not contain the books that should be written. Amen." (John 21:25)*

Imagine, for a moment, that you are an EMT responding to an emergency call. Someone is in need of emergency medical care and you must get to them before it is too late. Suppose you arrive on the scene with the siren blaring and lights flashing. You run into the house. One person is lying on the floor not moving. Another person is kneeling beside the person on the floor and several other people are standing around in the background. Would you run to the people standing around? Of course not. You would immediate look for the person in need of your help.

While Jesus was on this earth, He looked for those who were in need. If you were in a crowd of a thousand people where everyone was jumping with joy, and you were the only one weeping in tears, you would be the one He would seek out. He always sought out the wounded.

During the Vietnam War, a certain nurse was the subject of much discussion. After a battle, she would wander away from the medical camp onto the battlefield itself. Sometimes she would personally drag in a soldier who was in desperate need of medical attention. More than once she was reprimanded by the doctors. They told her she had no business on the battlefield. One day after a big battle, an officer saw her on the battlefield amid all the suffering and dying and death. He began to rebuke her: "What are you doing on that battlefield?" She said without hesitation, "I'm looking for the wounded. That's what I am here for." That nurse believed it was her solemn duty to find the wounded and bring them in where their wounds could be treated.

Maybe you have been wounded; not by gunfire or a car accident. Maybe you have been wounded spiritually. Can I tell you that Jesus cares? He understands your hurt. He understands your pain and He can help you if you will only let Him. In fact, He's been looking for you. He invites you to take the burden that you have been carrying around and give it to Him.

Casting all your care upon him; for he careth for you. (1 Pet 5:7)

Cast thy burden upon the LORD, and he shall sustain thee: he shall never suffer the righteous to be moved. (Ps. 55:22)

What many people do not realize is that all the heartaches, troubles, cruelty, unfairness, disease, suffering, and even death that we face on a daily basis is really all self-inflicted by mankind.

People want to blame God for their troubles. But it wasn't God who made Adam and Eve sin in the garden. In fact, He did everything He could do, short of taking away their free will, to prevent them from falling into sin. But just like us, Adam and Eve proved that, if left to ourselves, we will go after sin every time. It wasn't until sin came into this world that suffering and death came.

> *Wherefore, as by one man sin entered into the world, and death by sin; and so death passed upon all men, for that all have sinned: (Rom. 5:12)*

It is *our* sin that brought death into this world. But thank God, when Jesus came, He gave himself as payment for our sin so that we could live for eternity *without* sin!

CHAPTER 2

Watch Out for the Assailant!

It was almost 9:30 in the evening when police got a call. It was the 911 dispatcher notifying them of a possible burglary in progress with an injured victim at the scene.

Within minutes of arriving on the scene, police discovered the body of the homeowner, a doctor, lying in the hallway upstairs. He had been brutally murdered, apparently with a baseball bat that was found lying nearby.

Immediately the homicide detectives began searching every square inch of the house and property. They even brought in a police dog to sniff out possible evidence the police might overlook.

As they began the tedious task of trying to determine what had happened, none of them realized they were about to become involved in one of the most notorious murder cases of their small town's history.

After talking to neighbors, they were able to put together the events of the night. They determined that the doctor had left his office around 4:00 p.m. After he got home, he changed clothes and went outside to his front yard where he was seen using a baseball bat to drive a campaign sign into the ground. Based on the evidence, he then took a stepladder from the garage and carried it to the upstairs hallway where he removed a smoke detector from the ceiling.

It was at this point the surprise attack happened. Evidently he was surprised by someone who was already in the house. The unknown assailant grabbed the baseball bat and began beating the doctor unmercifully. But the attacker wasn't finished. After the doctor collapsed to the floor, the assailant continued their assault by stabbing him twice with a knife!

After the scene had been processed and the evidence had been examined, it was determined not to be a robbery. In fact, the evidence suggested that the doctor was brutally murdered by someone he knew. In other words, it was an inside job!

An attack in your own home is almost unthinkable. Your home is your haven. It is a place where you should feel the safest.

Over and over again the Bible reminds us to watch out for the assailant. No, it's not talking about someone lurking outside your living room window. It is talking about Satan, the most devious adversary of all.

The Bible warns us that we should watch out for Satan just like we would watch out for a wild lion loose in the woods where we were walking.

Be sober, be vigilant; because your adversary the devil, as a roaring lion, walketh about, seeking whom he may devour: (1 Pet. 5:8)

Satan is after you! He is after your marriage! He is after your home! He is after your children!

The problem is that many people do not see the danger. They do not really see him as a threat. They see Satan as the soft, furry, lion that is lazily laying around on the other side of the fence at the zoo. What they fail to realize is that lazy, cute-looking animal would "come alive" if you jumped over the fence in there with him!

I remember the last time we took our family to the zoo. My wife and I were walking by the area where the lions were. I vividly remember as I walked up, one particular lion caught my eye. He was looking right at me. That would have been fine except for the fact that he never STOPPED looking at me!

Even as we began to walk on by, that lion followed me with his eyes the entire time. It was as if he was saying, "Yeah, you think you're bad, don't you. Why do you just step in here with *me* for a minute and I'll *show* you who's bad!" I didn't *have* to climb over that fence to see how dangerous that lion was. He convinced me with just his eyes that I better watch my back!

What some people do to themselves is terrible. What society will sometimes do to people is bad. But the worst thing of all is what SATAN does to people. HE IS UNMERCIFUL! That is why the Bibles says we should be alert to his tactics. We should watch out for his attacks.

Since the Bible likens Satan to a lion, I wanted to find out how lions hunt. I began looking up information about lions and found some interesting things about how a lion hunts its prey. I found out that lions are stealthy. They will get as close to their prey as possible and even walk very casually until they are close enough to attack.

Satan is very much the same way. Because he is sneaky and devious, there are several things he wants to do.

Satan wants to DISTRACT us

Satan is smart. If he can't STOP you, he at least wants to SIDE-TRACK you. Many Christians have allowed themselves to be side-tracked by Satan. They used to pray every day but they've been side-tracked by others things. They used to attend church, they used to serve God, but they just can't find the time now.

He detours us by getting us so busy doing GOOD things, we forget the MAIN thing. He wants to keep us so busy with good causes we

16

have no time to seek the power of God in our life. We allow other things to steal away our love for the Lord.

The Apostle Paul had a close friend forsake him in the ministry because of his love for the world. He said in 2 Timothy 4:10, *"For Demas hath forsaken me, having loved this present world..."*

Many Christians have forsaken the Lord for the same reason. At one time I thought it was because no one wanted to be committed to anything anymore. But I finally realized that is not true. It's not that people aren't willing to be committed; it's that they are committed to the wrong things. And it's not always *bad* things, either.

Yes, it is true that many have allowed Satan to detour them by allowing themselves to become a slave to many sinful things such as drugs, alcohol or pornography. But there are many others who are patting themselves on the back right now because they are not involved in those particular sins, but haven't realized that they have gotten just as side-tracked by Satan doing *good* things.

How can you tell if you have been side-tracked by Satan? It is easy to tell when someone has become a slave to something other than Jesus Christ. As soon as there is a conflict between what *they* want to do and going to church, Christ and the church loses out.

"But Preacher, you've got to understand. I already made a commitment." What about your commitment to the Lord when you got saved? Why do we honor our commitment to the world over our commitment to God?

Watch out for the assailant! He wants to *distract* you.

Satan wants to DECEIVE us

The deceptive thing about Satan's attacks is that many times we never see them as an attack. When Satan came to Eve in the Garden of Eden, the reason she was willing to follow his lies was because she really didn't see them as a threat. The threat was not immediately recognized as such. I can guarantee you that when Satan first met Eve in the Garden, the conversation *didn't* go like this:

"Hello there, ma'am.

"Oh, Hello. I didn't know animals could talk."

"Well, you see, I'm not just *any* animal. I'm a

18

serpent. To be more specific, I am a fallen angel inside a serpent's body."

"OK, that didn't help me any because I don't even know what a fallen angel is."

"Well, let me introduce myself. My name is Satan. Some people call me Lucifer. Others call me Beelzebub, the Prince of Darkness, the Evil one, the Father of lies, the Tempter, and my personal favorite: the Wicked one. And how might you be on this fine, sunny day in this beautiful garden?"

"I'm great. Couldn't be better. What can I do for you?"

"Me? Well, it's not about what YOU can do for ME. It's about what I can do for YOU."

"And what *can* you do for me?"

"Well, I just happen to be able to offer you, for a limited time only, the biggest opportunity to come your way since you were just a rib! Why there has never been a bigger thing since the creation of dirt, I tell you."

"Hmm. Sounds interesting. Go on."

"Well, ma'am, it all started while I was in

Heaven."

"Oh, you got to live in the presence of God, too? Isn't He just wonderful?"

"Uh...wonderful? Yes. I mean, no!"

"I'll bet you just hated to leave, didn't you?"

"Hated? Well, you could say I hated, alright."

"So, tell me, why would anyone decide to leave the presence of such a wonderful God?"

"Well, you see...I didn't exactly *decide* to leave. I was, how can I say this, relocated against my will. Yes, that's it."

"Wow. That must have put a damper on the 'ole self-esteem I bet."

"You have no idea. Wait a minute. You're getting me off the subject. I'm trying to tell you about this wonderful opportunity I have for you."

"Yes, please continue."

"Now, about this opportunity, I am offering you a chance to follow me and about a third of the other angels who followed me and were...um...relocated, too."

"And, just why would I want to follow you and these other banished beings?"

20

"Why? To get away from such a mean and terrible God, that's why."

"Hmmm. Let's see. He gave me life, a loving husband, and a beautiful place to live in a perfect environment. Then, if that weren't enough, I get to enjoy it all in a perfect body that will never become starved, scarred, sick or saggy! Tell me again why I would want to leave Him to follow you."

"Well sure, all of that SOUNDS good...if you like that sort of thing. But follow me and I can promise you so much more. I promise you more pain, more suffering, more crying, more fear and more disappointment than you could ever imagine. And as a bonus—Hell for all eternity!"

No. Satan would have never approached Eve like that. And he will not approach YOU that way, either. He doesn't want you to know his agenda. He doesn't want you to see his motives. And he certainly doesn't want you to expose him for what he really is.

So how does he deceive us? The same way he deceived Eve in the Garden. He didn't try to convince Eve to follow HIM. He simply convinced Eve to follow Eve.

"Follow Eve? I don't understand" you say. It's simple. He just wanted Eve to follow her *own* desires because as long as she was following *her* desires, she couldn't be following *God's* desire for her.

And here's the really sneaky part of Satan's plan. Are you ready for this? Everyone who rejects Jesus Christ as their Savior and dies in their sin will spend eternity in Hell. But every one of them will go there by following *themselves*, not Satan!

Think about it. No one can blame Satan for the fact that they rejected Christ because he cannot force anyone to do anything. So, for all eternity, Satan will sit back and laugh at those doomed souls knowing they did it to themselves.

Satan wants to DEVOUR us.

1 Peter 5:8 says Satan is *"as a roaring lion, walketh about, seeking whom he may devour:"* The word *"devour"* means "to drink down" or "swallow up."

This reminds me of a young man named Daniel who was cast into a den of lions for praying to God. Notice what it says about the lions.

And the king commanded, and they brought those men which had accused Daniel, and they cast them into the den of lions, them, their children, and their wives; and **the lions had the mastery of them, and brake all their bones in pieces or ever they came at the bottom of the den.** *(Dan. 6:24)*

The word *"mastery"* means "to have power over" or "to rule over." That is Satan's goal: to swallow us up by ruling over our lives. He wants to chew us up and spit us out! When we stay away from the Bible and stay off our knees and stay away from church, we are allowing Satan to rule our lives.

Instead of allowing Satan to have the mastery over us, we should let the Master have the mastery! The Bible says, *"No man can serve two masters..."* (Matt. 6:24). Whichever one you give in to will be the master or ruler in your life.

Know ye not, that to whom ye yield yourselves servants to obey, his servants ye are to whom ye obey... (Rom. 6:16)

That is exactly what an addiction is. It is when a person continually gives in to a substance or

23

desire and as a result, it becomes their master. It rules their life.

One of the biggest ways in which Satan devours us is simple enough. It is by using the same thing that was *his* downfall—pride. Pride is a terrible thing. So terrible that it caused Satan to be kicked out of Heaven. And he will try to use your pride to be your downfall, too!

Pride goeth before destruction, and an haughty spirit before a fall. (Prov. 16:18)

Pride has destroyed a lot of lives. There is nothing wrong with thinking highly of ourselves, but the Bible warns us against thinking TOO HIGHLY of ourselves.

For I say, through the grace given unto me, to every man that is among you, not to think of himself more highly than he ought to think... (Rom. 12:3)

Seest thou a man wise in his own conceit? there is more hope of a fool than of him. (Prov. 26:12)

"..there is more hope of a fool than of him" means there is more hope for a profane sinner than for a self-righteous person. Why? Jesus said

24

in Mark 2:17, *"...I came not to call the righteous, but sinners to repentance."* The sinner knows he's a sinner and therefore sees his need for a Savior. The self-righteous person does not see himself as that bad. As a result, he doesn't see his need for Christ because he thinks he is good enough already.

Some are so puffed up in pride, they walk around like they are God's gift to the world. They walk around like super DUDES but they are really super DECEIVED! And after DECEPTION comes DESTRUCTION!

You realize that when we do not attend church we are really exhibiting pride in our life? We are saying that we are spiritual enough to not need preaching and teaching. We are not as weak as those other people.

That reminds me of a story I heard about a farmer who went to church every Sunday. After every service, as he shook the preacher's hand, he would say, "You sure gave it to 'em today, preacher!"

No matter what the preacher preached on, the farmer would still always say the same thing. One cold, wintery Sunday, because of the heavy snow no one was able to get to church except the preacher and that old farmer who came on his tractor.

"Finally," the preacher said to himself, "this time he will have to know the sermon was for him."

Well, the preacher preached the hottest sermon he had preached in a while. He preached on everything he knew that old farmer was guilty of doing. He finished his sermon; dismissed the service and waited for the farmer to come shake his hand. He couldn't wait to her what he had to say about *this* sermon.

Sure enough, the farmer walked up to the preacher, shook his hand and said, "Preacher, you sure gave it to 'em today, if they'd only been here to hear it."

You know what kept that farmer from seeing his own need for the Bible, and what keeps people today from seeing their need as well? P-R-I-D-E!

Did you know that all sin can be traced back to pride, which opens the door for a host of other sins? C.S. Lewis said, "Pride is the complete anti-God state of mind." A proud person wants all the attention and all the praise. But when you live for the glory, then you are competing against God and you will lose!

I am the LORD: that is my name: and my glory will I not give to another, neither my praise to graven images. (Isa. 42:8)

Proud people do not think they need anyone, especially God. But God said just the opposite.

Because thou sayest, I am rich, and increased with goods, and have need of nothing; and knowest not that thou art wretched, and miserable, and poor, and blind, and naked: (Rev. 3:17)

Some churches are so blessed they have even gotten away from their dependence upon God. They feel they no longer need Him. They are self-sufficient. That is why their services are dead— Christ is not a part of that church.

I remember one time, when I was a little boy, I went to a funeral with my mom and dad. Since my dad was a preacher and my mom and dad both sang together, we went to a lot of funerals.

This one particular funeral was in a church that seemed like it was so old that Noah must have built it after he got off the ark! It was so old that it didn't have indoor plumbing. No bathroom…did I mention I was a little boy? Did I mention that little boys have to go to the bathroom often? Well, right there in the middle of the funeral it hit me. I had to go! My mom couldn't take me out because they had to take part in the funeral so she broke the cardinal rule of parents with little boys who have to go to the bathroom in the middle of a funeral…she sent me by myself!

I climbed over the back of the pews to make my way out. "Why didn't you just walk out," you ask? I was a little boy. Climbing over the pews was much more adventurous!

Anyway, I made my way out the side door of the church and found what I considered to be the nearest "out-house." Everyone else would call it a tree. I finished and returned to the church only to find I had locked myself out! I couldn't get back in.

You would think that I would have sat down and quietly waited until the funeral was over, wouldn't you? You would be wrong. Did I mention that I was a little boy?

There was no way a locked door was going to

stay between me and a mountain of pews just waiting to be scaled again. So I began knocking, and knocking loudly I did! When the knocking didn't seem to work, I began yelling. I yelled, "Hey, would somebody please let me in?"

Did you know that is how Jesus feels in most churches?

Behold, I stand at the door, and knock: if any man hear my voice, and open the door, I will come in to him, and will sup with him, and he with me. (Rev. 3:20)

In this verse, Christ is not talking about standing at the door of the sinner's heart, He is standing outside the door of the church wanting to get in! What is keeping Him from entering many churches? P-R-I-D-E!

Someone said, "Pride is the only disease that makes everyone else sick but the one who has it!" The way we avoid pride is through humility. 1 Peter 5:5 says we are to be *"clothed in humility."* In fact, the Bible promises a great reward for the humble.

By humility and the fear of the LORD are riches, and honour, and life. (Prov. 22:4)

Why is pride so dangerous? Because it pits us against God.

But he giveth more grace. Wherefore he saith, God resisteth the proud, but giveth grace unto the humble. (James 4:6)

Do you want God to RESIST you or REWARD you? If you do not want to allow Satan to distract, deceive or devour you, you better watch out for the assailant!

CHAPTER 3

Look Out! He's Got A Weapon!

Satan is out to get you and he's got an arsenal of weapons at his disposal. While there are many different weapons Satan uses, we will look at only a few.

Weapon #1 – DISCOURAGEMENT

In 1 Kings 18, Elijah experienced a great spiritual victory. He won a face-to-face confrontation with eight hundred and fifty prophets of Baal, proving that he served the one, true God. This was one of the greatest spiritual experiences he had ever faced in his ministry.

When word got back to the wicked Queen Jezebel, she sent a message to him saying, "Elijah, by tomorrow I will make sure you are like the prophets you just killed." His great victory was short-lived. He was already facing opposition from Satan.

You need to realize that any time you take a stand for God and make progress for Him, Satan will begin attacking you. So, Elijah got scared and fled to the wilderness. Imagine, the great Elijah that stood boldly against eight hundred and fifty false prophets is now running from one woman!

When we see him again, he is sitting under a juniper tree defeated, discouraged, and disillusioned with the whole situation. Why was he being threatened? Had he not done the right thing up on Mount Carmel?

Understand that it wasn't his circumstances or what Jezebel said to him that had gotten him discouraged. It was what he THOUGHT about his circumstances that got him discouraged. His thoughts were defeating him more than what was happening around him.

Messed up thinking

Satan could not stop Elijah from having a great victory, but he messed up his thinking to the point that he could not enjoy his victory. The Bible says in 1 Corinthians 15:57 that, as believers, we have victory through Jesus Christ right now: *"But thanks be to God, which giveth us the victory through our Lord Jesus Christ."* Satan cannot take away our victory in Jesus Christ, but we can allow him to ruin our thinking so that we cannot enjoy a victorious life. The Devil majors on negative thinking. He loves to get believers thinking like unbelievers.

Someone said that when trials and opposition come, many Christians come down with a mild case of atheism. They are saved people but they are thinking like lost people. They believe in God but they think like an atheist! They know there is a God but doubt that He is really in control of their situation.

Isn't it funny how we can trust God for the biggest thing of all, saving our soul, but we have a difficult time trusting Him in lesser matters? What took place when you got saved was the greatest miracle you will ever experience. If you can trust God with your eternity, you can definitely trust Him with anything that happens in *this* life.

That is what Paul told Timothy in 2 Timothy 1:12, *"I know whom I have believed, and am persuaded that he is able to keep that which I have committed unto him against that day."* If you can commit your SOUL to Him, you can commit your CIRCUMSTANCES to Him.

It's a state of mind

Discouragement is a state of mind, not a set of circumstances. We know this is true because in all walks of life we see people who were able to overcome extremely negative circumstances and live victorious lives.

One such person was Bethany Hamilton. Born into a family of surfers on the island of Kauai, Hawaii, Bethany began surfing at a young age. At the age of eight, she entered her first surf competition. At the age of thirteen, the unthinkable happened. Bethany was attacked by a 14-foot tiger shark while surfing off Kauai's North Shore.

The attack left Bethany with a severed left arm.

34

By all accounts her surfing career was over. She would never surf again. But even after losing a large amount of her blood, and making it through several surgeries without infection, Bethany not only began to recover but did so with an unbelievably positive attitude.

Miraculously, just one month after the attack, Bethany returned to the water to continue pursuing her goal to become a professional surfer. In January of 2004, Bethany made her return to surf competition; placing 5th in the Open Women's division of that contest. With a powerful determination, Bethany continued to enter and excel in competition. Just over a year after the attack she took 1st place in the Explorer Women's division of the 2005 NSSA National Championships – winning her first National Title.

She could have easily given up while lying in that hospital room. She could have let thoughts of doubt and fear lead her into a pit of discouragement and depression that could have completely altered the course of her life. But she didn't! Her positive outlook helped bring her back.

Your circumstances will not cause you to be

discouraged but your THOUGHTS about your circumstances will.

Again, the Bible says that we are what we think. If I think defeated thoughts, I will be defeated. If I think negative thoughts, I will become negative. If, on the other hand, I think encouraging thoughts, I will become encouraged.

Think happy thoughts

We even see this in the life of Paul. In Acts 26, he had been arrested and brought before the king to answer for the charges brought against him. It didn't look very good. The circumstances were against him. The judicial system was against him.

There was really no reason for him to be encouraged with the situation whatsoever. But when the king let him speak, he said, *"I think myself happy, king Agrippa, because I shall answer for myself this day before thee touching all the things whereof I am accused of the Jews"* (Acts 26:2).

He could have said, "This is not fair. I am being railroaded here." He could have said, "I want my lawyer!" But instead he said, *"I think myself happy."*

36

One thing that stands out among the great giants of the faith is not that they faced no difficult circumstances, because we know they did. What stands out is the fact that they learned how to stay encouraged even in the most discouraging situations.

One problem many people have is that their happiness depends upon other people or upon better circumstances. They never seem to be in control of their own attitude. But when we allow our happiness to depend upon others, we will most likely stay in a valley of discouragement.

David, a man who often had more enemies than friends, did not leave his encouragement to chance. 1 Samuel 30:6 says,

> *"And David was greatly distressed; for the people spake of stoning him, because the soul of all the people was grieved, every man for his sons and for his daughters: but David encouraged himself in the LORD his God."*

The people were saying they wanted to stone David. These were discouraging circumstances to say the least! No wonder David was greatly distressed. He had every right to be discouraged, but he didn't let himself stay that way.

What did he do? Did he sit in the corner crying because there was no one to encourage him? No. The Bible says *"David encouraged himself in the LORD his God."* He could have tried to get encouragement through many different ways, but he realized the best way was to encourage himself *"in the LORD his God."*

Jesus said in John 16:33, *"These things I have spoken unto you, that in me ye might have peace. In the world ye shall have tribulation: but be of good cheer; I have overcome the world."* Notice that peace does not come from circumstances. Jesus said, *"in me ye might have peace."* True peace only comes from Jesus.

He then says that while we are living in this world we will have tribulations. Boy, that is encouraging, isn't it? Well, actually, He says we SHOULD be encouraged. *"But be of good cheer,"* He said. How? How can we be happy while going through tribulations? "Ah," he said. "That's easy. You can be happy because I have already overcome the world."

38

Weapon #2 – WORRY

One of the most destructive habits is also so common that many consider it as natural as breathing and as harmless as blinking. That habit is called worry. It is such a deceptive thief that its victims don't even know they've been robbed...of peace, of joy, of their time, and of emotional well-being.

What is worry?

In the New Testament, one Greek word translated as "worry" is *merimnao,* which means "to be anxious, to be distracted" or "to have a divided mind." To worry is to divide your mind between that which is useful and worthwhile and that which is damaging and destructive.

Jesus spoke of worrying in Matthew 6:27 when he said, *"Which of you by **taking thought** can add one cubit unto his stature?"* In other words, all the worrying in the world cannot change your stature or your situation in the least.

To begin with, let me say that there is hope! The very fact that Jesus Himself spoke about worry means that there are answers from God for your problem. We do not have to rely on man's opinions or ideas. As a believer, you have God's Word to teach you how to handle worry.

In Matthew 6, Jesus is speaking about worry. The encouraging thing is that He was speaking to His own followers! That should give you hope. Why? Because, if nothing else, it assures you that even believers can and do struggle with worry.

Worry is sinful

What does Jesus say about worry? In Matthew 6, He tells us no fewer than three times that it is wrong. Paul says the same thing in Philippians 4:6 when he said, *"Be careful for nothing;"*

Someone might ask, "If worry is so common, why is it sinful? Besides, doesn't it show that we are concerned about things in life? Isn't it better to worry a little than to be indifferent to the world around us?"

Jesus answers these questions in Matthew, chapter 6. He not only says it is wrong; He gives us reasons why it is wrong. Worry is wrong because its underlying nature is:

Disbelief—Worry reveals that you really don't believe God when He says He will provide all that you need. Worry is basically a negative view of the future. If you are a worrier, you are spending time speculating on what may or may not happen and then fearing the worst. Jesus tells us in Matthew 6:25-30:

> *Therefore I say unto you, Take no thought for your life, what ye shall eat, or what ye shall drink; nor yet for your body, what ye shall put on. Is not the life more than meat, and the body than raiment? 26 Behold the fowls of the air: for they sow not, neither do they reap, nor gather into barns; yet your heavenly Father feedeth them. Are ye not much better than they? 27 Which of you by taking thought can add one cubit unto his stature? 28 And why take ye thought for raiment? Consider the lilies of the field, how they grow; they toil not, neither do they spin: 29 And yet I say unto you, That even Solomon in all his glory was not arrayed like one of these. 30 Wherefore, if God so clothe the grass of the field, which to day is, and to morrow is cast into the oven, shall he not much more clothe you, O ye of little faith?*

Disbelief ultimately stems from a lack of faith. As unbelief gets the upper hand in our hearts, the result is anxiety. So the antidote for worry is to trust in God.

Disobedience—Worry reveals that you are taking on personal responsibility and concern for that which God has already promised to provide. Matthew 6:31-33 says:

> *Therefore take no thought, saying, What shall we eat? or, What shall we drink? or, Wherewithal shall we be clothed? 32 (For after all these things do the Gentiles seek:) for your heavenly Father knoweth that ye have need of all these things. 33 But seek ye first the kingdom of God, and his righteousness; and all these things shall be added unto you.*

Worry often causes us to act in disobedience by trying to obtain (our way) the things God promised to supply.

Destruction—Worry destroys your physical body, which is the temple of the Holy Spirit. Paul said in 1 Corinthians 6:19-20, *"What? know ye not that your body is the temple of the Holy Ghost which is in you, which ye have of God, and ye are not your own? For ye are bought with a price: therefore glorify God in your body, and in your spirit, which are God's."*

Worry is physically destructive because it can

bring about a host of physical ailments, such as high blood pressure, heart trouble, headaches, and other stomach disorders.

Dishonor—Worry shifts the focus of attention from the all sufficient power of Christ to your human insufficiency and insecurity. Ultimately, worry can undermine your Christian witness by presenting God as powerless and unworthy of praise.

The Bible says, *"Let your light so shine before men, that they may see your good works, and glorify your Father which is in heaven"* (Matt. 5:16).

Weapon #3 – GUILT

If you are battling with guilt, let me ask you, is it **good** guilt or **bad** guilt?

"What? Good guilt? I never knew there was such a thing as good guilt," you say. "What is the difference between good guilt and bad guilt?"

Good guilt is godly guilt. It is a loving tool of God used to convict, correct and conform your character when you go astray. Bad guilt is used by Satan that will overshadow you with feelings of shame and condemnation. Godly guilt is your friend. Godly guilt motivates you to repent and be free from your sin. But false guilt is a relentless foe. It is the enemy within that encourages not godly, but superficial sorrow that brings death!

Paul spoke of this in 2 Corinthians 7:9-10 when he said, *"Now I rejoice, not that ye were made sorry, but that ye sorrowed to repentance: for ye were made sorry after a godly manner...For godly sorrow worketh repentance to salvation not to be repented of: but the sorrow of the world worketh death."*

What is true guilt?

From earliest childhood, no one has escaped guilt. We experienced guilt when we stole a cookie or told a lie. True guilt is the result of sin. When we sin we are guilty, and a penalty must be paid for our sin so that fellowship with God can be restored.

After David committed adultery with Bathsheba, he repented and cried out to God, *"Against thee, thee only, have I sinned, and done this evil in thy sight"* (Ps. 51:4). Sin is first and foremost a sin against God and guilt is therefore a result of that sin. James 2:10 says, *"For whosoever shall keep the whole law, and yet offend in one point, he is guilty of all."*

How should I respond to guilt?

First: admit your sin. You experience true guilt when you recognize the fact that you have sinned. David was honest about his sin in Psalm 32:5: *"I acknowledged my sin unto thee, and mine iniquity have I not hid. I said, I will confess my transgressions unto the LORD; and thou forgavest the iniquity of my sin. Selah."*

How did God respond? He forgave David's sin and the good news is His response is the same for anyone who will confess their sin to Him.

The Bible says in 1 John 1:9, *"If we confess our sins, he is faithful and just to forgive us our sins, and to cleanse us from all unrighteousness."*

When the sin goes away, so does the guilt. In fact, the Bible says that when God forgives your sin, he removes it *"As far as the east is from the west"* (Ps. 103:12).

Weapon #4 – ANGER

Will Rogers said, "People who fly into a rage seldom make a good landing!" The Bible says, *"He that is soon angry dealeth foolishly: and a man of wicked devices is hated."* (Prov. 14:17).

Did you know that nothing good can come from a bad temper? James 1:20 says, *"For the wrath of man worketh not the righteousness of God."*

Someone defined anger as "A sudden explosion of madness." An angry man picks a fight but a man in control of his anger stops a fight. *"A wrathful man stirreth up strife: but he that is slow to anger appeaseth strife"* (Prov. 15:18). An angry man stirs up strife in the home. He stirs up strife in the church. He basically stirs up trouble wherever he goes because wherever he goes he takes is anger with him.

Proverbs 25:8 says, *"Go not forth hastily to strive, lest thou know not what to do in the end thereof, when thy neighbour hath put thee to shame."*

Notice the first part of that verse again. It says, *"Go not forth hastily to strive."* God says to be careful about having a short fuse and a quick temper. The next part says, *"...when thy neighbour hath put thee to shame."* Your neighbor knows you best. In fact, the closest neighbor you have is your spouse and family. No one lives any closer to you than they do. They see you when no one else does.

Proverbs 29:20 says, *"Seest thou a man that is hasty in his words? there is more hope of a fool than of him."* If there's one thing that really gets us into trouble it is being hasty with our words. You know that feeling that wells up inside you when you get angry and makes you want to tell someone off? The Bible says, it would be better for you to not say anything right then out of anger or you will say the wrong thing.

If you have a problem with anger, here are some things to do.

CONFESS it

Admit you have a problem with anger. Own up to it. But that is not all. Proverbs 29:22 says, *"An angry man stirreth up strife, and a furious man aboundeth in transgression."* Now, we've already seen that *"An angry man stirreth up strife,"* but this goes a step further. It has been said that when a person loses their temper, there is more to it than just what they are angry about.

That is what the Bible is saying here: *"a furious man aboundeth in transgression."*

See, it is a domino effect. There are other sins in this man's life than just anger. When a man gets angry and loses his temper at his wife because his toast is a little burnt, the toast is NOT the real issue there. There is more than meets the eye that has been simmering under the surface.

Since the Bible says that an angry man literally *"abounds"* in transgressions, there are probably other sins that need to be dealt with before the anger will be resolved. 1 John 1:8, says, *"If we say that we have no sin, we deceive ourselves, and the truth is not in us."*

CONSIDER it

Proverbs 25:28 says, *"He that hath no rule over his own spirit is like a city that is broken down, and without walls."* A city that is without walls is without protection. They must consider what the lack of protection is doing to them and their families.

Likewise, an angry man must consider what harm his anger is doing to himself, his family and his relationship with God.

CONTROL it

Proverbs 29:11 says, *"A fool uttereth all his mind: but a wise man keepeth it in till afterwards."* Some people will give you a piece of their mind and they usually don't have much to spare!

They say, "Well I just speak my mind." That's not always a good thing. Remember the old saying: "It is better to keep your mouth shut and be thought a fool, than to open your mouth and remove all doubt!"

The last part of that verse says, *"a wise man keepeth it in till afterwards."* I can't tell you how many times that waiting a while before I responded to something has saved me considerable embarrassment. That is scriptural. You don't utter all of your mind. You wait until you have calmed down and can think straight.

"Well, I just can't control my anger, preacher." sure you can. I can prove it. You get into a big argument and you raise your voice in anger then all the sudden the phone rings and you say in a calm voice, "Hello? Hi, preacher! Why we were just sitting her re-enacting the Sermon on the Mount. Honey, you can get down off the table now." What did you do? You instantly controlled your so-called uncontrollable temper.

One of the best ways to avoid having a problem with anger is by not becoming friends with a person who has a problem with anger. Why? Because the Bible teaches us that our friends will influence our behavior.

> *Make no friendship with an angry man; and with a furious man thou shalt not go: Lest thou learn his ways, and get a snare to thy soul. (Prov. 22:24-25)*

That's not all, folks!

This is not all of Satan's weapons. These were just a few that he will use against your mind. I go into more detail in my book *What Are You Thinking?* But the next time Satan begins to attack you, keep these things in mind.

We must fight the flesh with the Spirit.

For though we walk in the flesh, we do not war after the flesh: (2 Cor. 10:3)

Many times we fail to control our thought lives because we try to fight the flesh with the flesh. We will never conquer our flesh using the world's methods. David said in Psalm 1:1-2, *"Blessed is the man that walketh not in the counsel of the ungodly, nor standeth in the way of sinners, nor sitteth in the seat of the scornful. But his delight is in the law of the LORD; and in his law doth he meditate day and night."* In other words, the *"blessed"* or happy man is one who meditates on spiritual things, *"the law of the LORD."*

We must trust God's power to pull down the strongholds

> *For the weapons of our warfare are not carnal, but mighty through God to the pulling down of strong holds; (2 Cor. 10:4)*

While we are no match for the power of Satan by ourselves, he is no match for the power of God! Paul reminds us that we can accomplish anything through God's power. He said, *"I can do all things through Christ which strengtheneth me"* (Phil. 4:13)

We must reject (cast down) any thought that leads us to doubt God or His Word.

Casting down imaginations, and every high thing that exalteth itself against the knowledge of God... (2 Cor. 10:5a)

Though we have access to God's power, we are still responsible for rejecting the wrong thoughts, ourselves. That is our responsibility. Any thought that would cause us to doubt God or his Word must be rejected.

We must bring every thought captive by obeying Jesus Christ.

...and bringing into captivity every thought to the obedience of Christ; (2 Cor. 10:5b)

One of the best ways to avoid doing what is wrong is by doing what is right. In other words, the best way to guard against disobedience is through active obedience.

If you want to be victorious in defeating Satan's attacks on you, begin reading God's Word and obeying what it says.

CHAPTER 4

Do You Have A Pulse?

A Paramedic was asked on a local TV talk-show program: "What was your most unusual and challenging 911 call?"

"Recently," the paramedic began, we got a call from that big white church on Main Street. A frantic usher was very concerned that during their worship service an elderly man passed out in a pew and appeared to be dead. The usher could find no pulse and there was no noticeable breathing."

"What was so unusual about this particular

call?" the interviewer asked.

"Well," the paramedic said, "we carried out four guys before we found the one who was dead!"

That story would be funny if it weren't so close to the truth. Sadly, too many churches would fit that description. But that is not the way God intended for it to be. The church should be a place of life, not death.

Christianity is all about life. It is based on a living Savior Who has given us a living Book to live by. Someone has said, "The Bible is a living Book, written by a living God to teach us how to live life." If you believe the Bible, then you know there are two kinds of life: EARTHLY life and ETERNAL life.

Regarding the beginning of our earthly life, the Bible says that all life has its source in God. Consider these verses.

In the beginning God created the heaven and the earth. (Gen. 1:1)

So God created man in his own image, in the image of God created he him; male and female created he them. (Gen. 1:27)

And the LORD God formed man of the dust of the ground, and breathed into his nostrils the breath of life; and man became a living soul. (Gen. 2:7)

Regardless of what the public schools may teach, man did not come into being through some evolutionary process. I do not believe in a "Big Bang." I believe in a "Big God" Who made all things and by Whom all things consist.

The Bible says, *"The fool hath said in his heart, There is no God"* (Ps. 14:1). He says it in his heart because his head knows better. Anyone that has a brain that functions knows that for there to be a CREATION, there must be a CREATOR. I may have had descendants who swung from their **necks**, but I never had any who swung from their **tails**!

As you know, when a paramedic arrives on the scene of someone who is unconscious, one of the first things they check is the pulse. They are trying to determine if the person is alive or not. If you are reading this book, then I am sure that you have a pulse. It is obvious that you are alive. If not, I would stop reading this book and immediately seek help!

We all want to live and have a meaningful life because life is important to us. Well, life is also important to God. From the very first chapter of the first Book of the Bible, it talks about life. And the same Bible that tells us about EARTHLY life also tells us about ETERNAL life.

How Long Do You Have?

Some people act as though they will live forever. The truth is no one knows how long their lives will be on this earth. If you go to a cemetery you will see graves of all sizes. As a pastor, I have preached the funerals of the elderly and I've preached the funeral of the newborn. James 4:14 says, *"For what is your life? It is even a vapour, that appeareth for a little time, and then vanisheth away."*

Our lives are said to be a *"vapour."* That word means mist. Think of it this way. Have you ever been outside in the winter time and noticed when you exhale that you can see the mist from your breath? It appears for a moment, but then it is gone. That is exactly the way your life is. It is here one moment, and the next moment it is gone. David said, *"...there is but a step between me and death."* (1 Sam. 20:3)

"But, preacher, I am healthy. I will live to be a hundred years old." Wow! That would be some feat! I remember when I was young, I thought forty was old. Now I have come to realize that "old" is simply whatever age that I am not yet at! Sure, a hundred years old *is* a long time. But have you ever thought about a hundred years compared to eternity? It is like comparing a molecule of water to all the oceans in the world. There's really no comparison.

You and I will not live long on this earth because life is short.

One Life to Live

James 4:14 doesn't say, "What is your lives," plural. It says, *"For what is your life,"* singular. You only get one. Reincarnation is not a biblical teaching. We cannot come back as a cow or animal or another human being.

A great example of this is found in 2 Samuel 12 where David's son died. In (v.23) David said, *"But now he is dead, wherefore should I fast? can I bring him back again? I shall go to him, but he shall not return to me."* David was not expecting his son to come back as some other life form.

Another verse that also illustrates this is 2 Samuel 14:14 which says, *"For we must needs die, and are as water spilt on the ground, which cannot be gathered up again..."* But I believe the best verse that teaches against reincarnation is Hebrews 9:27 which says, *"And as it is appointed unto men once to die, but after this the judgment:"* The Bible doesn't say, "but after this comes another life and then another life and then another one."

You have been given but one life and this one life is fragile. You do not know when death is going to come knocking on your door. You might miss your doctor's appointment or have to reschedule that oil change, but death is an appointment you will not be late for. Death is no respecter of persons.

Death didn't care that she was a 6-year-old beauty queen in the state of Colorado. When it was time, death came with wicked hands and strangled the life out of JonBenet Ramsey. Death didn't care that he was the King of Rock-N-Roll. Death claimed the life of Elvis Presley. Death didn't care that she was the world's Princess, known and loved by millions. When her time came, death took the life of Princess Diana.

And friend, death is hot on your trail, too!

The BIG Question.

The big question is what are you going to do with this short life? What are you going to do to make sure your life counts for something when you are gone? What *are* your plans? That is a big question, isn't it? But an even bigger question is how does God fit into your plans?

The average person is living today saying, "I will do this" and "I plan to do that." They have all these plans for their life and few, if any of those plans, ever include God! Basically, they are living their life EXEMPTING God, when they should be EXALTING God.

Our big mistake is trying to "fit" God into our plans instead of living His plan for us. The most dangerous thing you can do is exclude God. Remember what happened to the rich farmer in the Book of Luke 12?

And he spake a parable unto them, saying, The ground of a certain rich man brought forth plentifully: And he thought within himself, saying, What shall I do, because I

911...What Your Emergency?

have no room where to bestow my fruits?
And he said, This will I do: I will pull down
my barns, and build greater; and there will
I bestow all my fruits and my goods. And I
will say to my soul, Soul, thou hast much
goods laid up for many years; take thine
ease, eat, drink, and be merry. But God said
unto him, Thou fool, this night thy soul shall
be required of thee: then whose shall those
things be, which thou hast provided? (Luke
12:16-20)

This man was no doubt a shrewd business man. If he were alive today, he would have probably been on the cover of *Forbes Magazine* as businessman of the year. This man lived life to its fullest, but he lived life for himself. It was all about him and what he wanted out of life with no concern for God whatsoever.

The business world no doubt thought a lot of him. What did God think of Him? Surely God was impressed with his business mind, right? Nope! He said, *"Thou fool."* God said that a person who runs around living their life without any thought of God or His Word is a FOOL!

This man was wise when it came to his goods, but he was foolish when it came to God. He thought he had invested it all and had it secure, but when death comes it doesn't matter.

There is a saying: "He who dies with the most toys wins." But there is another saying: "He who dies with the most toys is still dead!"

Don't be a fool. You know what a fool is? A fool is a person who has planned out his LIFE but not planned out his AFTER-LIFE. It is a person who lives for the TEMPORAL and not for the ETERNAL. This man was rich and had more than he could ever need, yet he died a fool's death.

For what shall it profit a man, if he shall gain the whole world, and lose his own soul? (Mark 8:36)

You can live your life and plan your vacations and raise your children without putting God into the equation, but when you die you'll be the biggest fool who ever lived. You not only will have lost the possessions you lived to gain, but you will have lost your soul, too!

What are you doing with this life God has given you? What are you living life for? What is the goal of your life? Is it to make more money? Have a nice retirement? Get that dream home?

"Okay, preacher. You win. I give up. Tell me, what IS the purpose of life?" you say.

Wouldn't it be great to have the wisest man in all the world give us the answer? We can! Solomon was the wisest man who ever lived. He wrote three books: Proverbs, Ecclesiates and Song of Solomon.

Solomon had every imaginable thing a man could want, but by time he had come to the end of his life, he began to see all the mistakes he had made and how foolish they were. He finally came to the conclusion of the whole purpose of man.

Let us hear the conclusion of the whole matter: Fear God, and keep his commandments: for this is the whole duty of man. (Ecc. 12:13)

In other words, if you go through this life and do not learn to fear God and keep His commandments, you haven't lived...you've just existed!

CHAPTER 5

30 Seconds After You Die

"If it is true that a man will die one day, what then" you ask? That is a very good question. Job asked the same question when he said, *"But man dieth, and wasteth away: yea, man giveth up the ghost, and where is he?"* (Job 14:10).

When God made you, He made you a living soul but one day you will die. Thirty seconds after you die (if you die without Christ as your Savior) there are three things you will know for sure.

1. Hell is real

In Luke, chapter 16, the Bible tells about the death of a rich man who rejected God. In verses 22-23 it says,

> *And it came to pass, that the beggar died, and was carried by the angels into Abraham's bosom: the rich man also died, and was buried; 23) And in hell he lift up his eyes, being in torments, and seeth Abraham afar off, and Lazarus in his bosom.*

Thirty seconds after you die without Christ, you will realize what the rich man found and that is that Hell is real!

Hell is a place of no more Changes

While on this Earth, you are free to make any changes you like. If you do not like a certain restaurant, you can change your mind and go to another one. If you do not like your neighborhood, you can change where you live.

But friend, if you find yourself in Hell, there will be no more changes.

You will not be able to change who you are with. The Bible identifies the people who will be your neighbors in Hell.

> *But the fearful, and unbelieving, and the abominable, and murderers, and whoremongers, and sorcerers, and idolaters, and all liars, shall have their part in the lake which burneth with fire and brimstone: which is the second death. (Rev 21:8)*

You will not be able to change where you are at. Once you take your last breath, your eternity is sealed. There is no changing your fate.

Hell is a place of no more Chances

There will be no more chances to accept Christ as your Savior and get out. There will be no more chances to warn others of that terrible fate.

2. The Devil lied.

The second thing you will realize thirty seconds after you die is that the Devil lied to you! He lied when he told you that there is no such thing as life after death. The Bible tells us that after death comes the judgment.

> *And as it is appointed unto men once to die, but after this the judgment: (Heb. 9:27)*

You will also realize that the Devil lied to you when He told you that Hell was just the grave. The Bible says that after the rich man died, *"in hell he lift up his eyes, being in torments..."* (Luke 16:23). Over and over again, the Bible describes the pain and torment associated with Hell and the Lake of Fire. It is a real place. Since I have given a much more detailed description of Hell in my book *The 5 Most Disturbing Things About Hell,* I will only say that as surely as there is a beautiful Heaven, the Bible says there is a literal burning Hell.

The wicked shall be turned into hell, and all the nations that forget God. (Psalm 9:17)

And death and hell were cast into the lake of fire. This is the second death. And whosoever was not found written in the book of life was cast into the lake of fire. (Rev. 20:14-15)

3. There is no way out!

And the devil that deceived them was cast into the lake of fire and brimstone, where the beast and the false prophet are, and shall be tormented day and night for ever and ever. (Rev. 20:10)

"But, there must be a better way," you say. There is! Jesus said, *"I am the way, the truth, and the life: no man cometh unto the Father, but by me"* (John 14:6).

Eternal life is not earned through good works or church membership. Eternal life comes only from realizing that you are a sinner and because of your sin, God cannot allow you into Heaven.

You must repent and turn from trying to get to Heaven YOUR way. Pray and tell Jesus you realize that you are a sinner and need His forgiveness.

There are NO magical words or phrases that will save a person. Salvation comes when you believe, by faith, that Jesus died on the cross, was buried, and He rose again on the third day to pay for your sin.

"But I don't even know HOW to pray," you say. That's OK. God sees the desire of your heart.

Just talk to Him from your heart and tell Him that you realize you are a sinner and don't deserve to go to Heaven and by faith you are placing your trust in Him, and Him alone, to forgive your sin and take you to Heaven when you die.

That's it! Simple isn't it? God didn't make salvation complicated. He just wants you to give Him 100% of your heart and trust Him for your salvation.

CONCLUSION

Remember at the beginning of the book I told you about the young model who walked into the propeller? Here's what you might not have known.

A report released by the National Transportation Safety Board showed that the pilot warned the young lady to be careful of the plane's spinning propeller. He tried to direct her to exit towards the rear of the plane. Evidently she was warned but did not heed the warning.

Can I ask you a question? Will that be you, one day? Will you stand before God at the Judgment and have to explain why you were warned about Hell, but refused to heed the warning?

If you are not certain about your salvation, I beg you not to put off any longer. Trust in Jesus Christ today! Right now!

About The Author

Mark Agan has been in the ministry for over thirty years. He has pastored churches in Georgia, Florida, and now in North Carolina, where he currently pastors. He is also the Chaplain for the Chatham County Sheriff's Office in Chatham County, North Carolina.

To learn more about the author, visit his web site at: **www.MarkAgan.com**

Other Books By Mark Agan

The Deceptive Side Of Suicide

The Power of Meditating On Scripture

What Are You Thinking? Winning the Battle Of Your Mind

Keeping It All Together When It's All Falling Apart

How To Make Your Prayer Time Fresh & Exciting!

...and others are available on
www.Amazon.com.

Made in the USA
Middletown, DE
21 September 2021